Peace in Paul and Luke

Michael J Gorman

Raymond E Brown Professor of Biblical Studies and
Theology, St Mary's Seminary and University
Baltimore, Maryland, USA

GROVE BOOKS LIMITED
RIDLEY HALL RD CAMBRIDGE CB3 9HU

Contents

Notes
This booklet is adapted, with the permission of the publishers, from 'The (New) Covenant of Peace,' chapter six of Michael J Gorman, 'The Death of the Messiah and the Birth of the New Covenant: A (Not So) New Model of the Atonement' (Eugene, OR: Cascade, 2014).

Acknowledgments
I am grateful to Ian Paul and Michael Thompson for the invitation to write this booklet, and to the folks at Wipf and Stock Publishers for their support of the project.

First Impression June 2015
ISSN 1365–490X
ISBN 978 1 85174 939 3

The New Covenant of Peace According to Paul and Luke

Many Christians would be quick to say that 'peace' is an important Christian word; indeed, that it is a gift of God in Christ (Luke 2.14), the result of justification via Jesus' death (Rom 5.1), part of the fruit of the Spirit (Gal 5.22), and a necessity for healthy church life (Eph 4.3). But it is worth wondering whether the church has made peace and peacemaking as central to its life as it is in Scripture.

Of particular interest to us in this booklet is the theme of peace in the writings of Paul and Luke. We focus on these biblical authors in part because peace is a prominent theme in each, and in part because both Paul and Luke employ the term 'new covenant' in association with the promise of God fulfilled in Jesus, especially through his death. For them, the promised new covenant that has arrived in Jesus is also the covenant of peace. And the people of the new covenant are, therefore, God's peace-filled and peaceable people.

The Promised Covenant of Peace

Students of the Scriptures of Israel are familiar with the promise of Jeremiah that God would bring about a new covenant and a new-covenant community (Jer 31.31–34). But similar prophetic promises highlight the permanent and peaceful character of that future reality:

> For the mountains may depart and the hills be removed, but my steadfast love shall not depart from you, and my covenant of peace shall not be removed, says the Lord, who has compassion on you. (Isa 54.10)
>
> I will make with them a covenant of peace and banish wild animals from the land, so that they may live in the wild and sleep in the woods securely. (Ezek 34.25)
>
> I will make a covenant of peace with them; it shall be an everlasting covenant with them; and I will bless them and multiply them, and will set my sanctuary among them forevermore. (Ezek 37.26)[1]

These three occurrences of the phrase 'covenant of peace' point us to a fundamental dimension of the new covenant, and of the New Testament writings, that is generally under-appreciated and under-explored. Moreover, the Christian tradition, even when it has focused on participation in Jesus' death, has too often failed to make the connection between a spirituality of participation in that death and a spirituality of peace. Nonetheless, although the precise phrase 'covenant of peace' does not appear in the New Testament, Paul and Luke make the covenant of peace and the corollary 'way of peace' (which phrase they *do* use) central to their theological project. And they connect peace to Jesus' death.

But not everyone has noticed this focus on peace in Paul and Luke.

The Absence of Peace in New Testament Studies

It is rather odd how relatively little attention is paid by most people, including many scholars, to the theme of peace in the Bible generally, and in Paul and Luke specifically. There may be good reasons for this, particularly if one only looks at the actual occurrences of *eirēnē* (peace) and cognates in the two authors. Forty-three occurrences of the noun, and four of related verbs, in the Pauline correspondence, and only twenty-one occurrences of the noun in Luke-Acts, might not seem significant. However, importance is determined not only by the quantity of texts, but also by such factors as their location, their connection to related words and themes in the author's corpus, their relationship to scriptural texts and motifs, and so on. Any or all of these could either reinforce or challenge an initial impression based solely on quantity.

Recent scholarship on Paul is something of a mixed bag on the topic of peace. Udo Schnelle (*Apostle Paul: His Life and Theology*) represents what seems to be the implicit attitude among many interpreters of Paul: that for Paul peace is a minor theme that (1) appears primarily at the beginning and end of his letters—liturgical, epistolary and hortatory flourishes, if you will, but little of great theological substance; and (2) elsewhere expresses a 'vertical' theology of reconciliation with God that is supplemented with a 'conventional' ethic, theologically grounded but having little if any specifically christological import.[2]

N T Wright, on the other hand, in his *magnum opus*, *Paul and the Faithfulness of God*, sees Pauline theology quite differently. Because he believes that for Paul Jesus is first of all the Jewish messiah, Wright repeatedly refers to the prophetic hope for an age of peace and justice, claiming that Paul believed that it had arrived—at least in some sense, though clearly not exactly as the prophets had hoped and equally clearly not in its fullness—through the death and resurrection of Jesus. Moreover, Wright argues that reconciliation is at the heart of Paul's own ministry and a cardinal mark of the church. With a number of other scholars, Wright believes that Paul's gospel of peace and justice challenges the Roman gospel of so-called peace and justice, but he insists that the origin of Paul's belief in this peace and justice is christological, or messianic: the prophetically promised peace and justice of the messianic age have arrived in Jesus.

> **Reconciliation is at the heart of Paul's own ministry and a cardinal mark of the church**

One would expect that peace would fare somewhat better in scholarship on Luke, but that is actually not generally the case. François Bovon's *Luke the Theologian*, largely a report on the history of research in various Lukan topics, occasionally notes that peace is part of Luke's soteriology. But peace receives no sustained attention, does not appear in the index, and is only mentioned once in the book's concluding broad survey of research. To Bovon's credit, however, he rightly insists that, though they are eschatological realities, 'Peace and kingdom in Luke never lose their earthly and political connotations,' and peace is a present reality, both in the Gospel of Luke and in Acts.[3]

Evangelical Darrell Bock's recent theology of Luke considers peace as one of the six 'benefits of salvation' in Luke's theology, but it receives only a brief paragraph of discussion and is defined solely as 'a reconciled relationship between God and humanity.'[4] This latter assessment is clearly in conflict with Bovon's 'earthly and political' interpretation and seems to reflect a theological bias more than the actual theology of Luke.

Much more promising is the work of Paul Borgmann, *The Way According to Luke: Hearing the Whole Story of Luke-Acts*. Borgmann posits 'the Way' as that which unites Luke and Acts both structurally and thematically. The 'Way of God' (Luke 20.21) is a summary phrase for Luke's reinterpretation of Scripture in light of Jesus, and it is 'synonymous with the Way of salvation, the kingdom of God, and the Way of peace.'[5] For Luke, argues Borgmann, the purpose of God promised to Abraham is to bring about universal *shalom*.

In his important book *Covenant of Peace*, Mennonite New Testament scholar Willard Swartley aims to correct the general inattention to peace in NT studies, including the writings of Paul and Luke. If, with scholars like Wright, Borgmann, and Swartley, we can see the centrality of peace to Paul and Luke—whose writings constitute more than 50% of the New Testament—we will be on our way to an understanding of the New Testament that properly foregrounds peace.

Some Questions and a Proposal

Even if it were true that Paul speaks of peace primarily, or only, in specific kinds of epistolary and liturgical contexts, would we want to dismiss the references as insignificant, since Paul often speaks of grace in the same breath? Moreover, as many commentators have noted, Paul's epistolary and liturgical excerpts do give voice to his conviction that in Christ God's *shalom* has arrived. But the apparent formulaic repetition of 'grace and peace' language, together with the apparent lack of theological development of the notion, often means that interpreters note the presence of peace/*shalom* and then move on to what are (supposedly) Paul's real concerns.

But what if 'grace and peace' is more essential, more central to what Paul is about? What if 'peace' is not merely inner calm, as in the popular imagination, or a relatively minor aspect of salvation? What if every Pauline letter is an exercise in reminding followers of Jesus that the gracious gift of the Messiah is the promised *shalom* of God?

In addition to the liturgical formulae, we have from Paul an initial sign that this is in fact the case in Rom 5.1–2: 'Therefore, since we are justified by faith, we have *peace* with God through our Lord Jesus Christ, through whom we have obtained access to this *grace* in which we stand.' This text suggests that 'peace with God,' equated also with reconciliation, is at the heart of Paul's gospel of grace (5.10–11). Moreover, rather than foreclosing a horizontal dimension to peace, its centrality to the gospel immediately raises the question, 'What does this peace with God have to do with the human condition of injustice and violence depicted in Rom 1.18–3.20, and with the pleas for harmony that run through chapters 9–11 and again through chapters 12–15?' And if Paul (or one of his disciples) calls Jesus 'the Lord of peace' (2 Thess 3.16, possibly alluding to Isa 60.17b), what does that mean for the role of peace in Pauline theology?

What does this peace with God have to do with the human condition of injustice?

Similarly, if one merely counts the occurrences of 'peace' in Luke's writings, one might conclude that it has a modest role in the Gospel of Luke and a minimal role in Acts. If, however, one considers other factors, one might come to a quite different conclusion. For instance, if Luke-Acts is thought of as a unified story, then at the very beginning of the story two major characters announce peace as the purpose of God's sending Jesus (Zechariah in 1.79 and the heavenly host in 2.14), while later on the central character in the first half of Acts, Peter, summarizes both the gospel narrative itself and the ongoing message of the apostolic gospel in these words: 'You know the message he sent to the people of Israel, *preaching [the good news of] peace by Jesus Christ*—he is Lord of all' (Acts 10.36). These announcements of peace are summative and programmatic statements of Luke's agenda—of *God's* agenda, in Luke's view. That is, the gospel is the gospel of peace, and the Lord of all is the Lord of peace.

The evidence is beginning to suggest that peace is a central and critical part of Pauline and Lukan theology about Christ and the community of the new covenant that he created. The new covenant that Jesus came to inaugurate as Messiah, and which he continues to administer as the resurrected Lord, is the covenant of peace. For Paul and for Luke, I suggest, Jesus is both the *source* and the *shape* of God's *shalom*. While this evidence demonstrates the centrality of peace and peacemaking to Pauline and Lukan Christology and soteriology, it also shows that Paul and Luke do not think of Christ as peacemaker in isolation, but only in conjunction with God the Father and the Spirit, on the one hand, and in union with the *ekklēsia* on the other.

Moreover, I would suggest as well that both Paul and Luke (as well as other New Testament writers) articulate their vision of peace as an alternative to the Roman Empire and the famous *pax Romana*. This *pax*—which was hardly established nonviolently—had several dimensions from an official Roman perspective: it was

a. the longed-for 'golden age' of peace and security, which had been

b. achieved and maintained by military victory and power over enemies and which

c. imposed Roman law and culture on the conquered, all

d. by the power, and with the approval, of the Roman gods.

The peace of Christ will be *quite* different.

The thesis which I am proposing, but which can only be sketched in this booklet, has three main aspects:

The promise of shalom fulfilled. For *Paul*, the prophetically promised age of eschatological, messianic peace has arrived in the death and resurrection of Jesus the Messiah, an age characterized especially by reconciliation and nonviolence. Jesus' death and resurrection were congruent with his teaching ministry. For *Luke*, the age of peace has also been inaugurated; for him it arrives not only in Christ's death and resurrection, but already in Jesus' birth and ministry, as well as his death, resurrection and exaltation, and in the gift of the Spirit. This new age is characterized by reconciliation and nonviolence, but also especially by justice marked by status-reversal and inclusion.

Shalom as the effect of the cross. For *Paul*, God in Christ, on the cross, has made peace with humanity and between humans. The centrality of peacemaking to atonement theology is characteristic of Paul, but it is also present in *Luke*.

Shalom as ongoing divine and messianic activity and as ecclesial identity marker. For *Paul*, Jesus is the present Lord of peace, active in his communities by the Spirit to continue making peace in and through them, especially through practices of unification and reconciliation internally, and nonretaliation and nonviolence externally. For *Luke*, Jesus came to create a new people who would walk in the way of peace, and this also defines the Spirit-filled church, 'the Way.'

Due to limitations of space, we will pay special attention to the first point.

4 The Promised Prince of Peace and the Covenant of Peace: Isaiah and Ezekiel 'in Concert'[6]

Jewish New Testament scholar Mark Nanos believes the Christ-followers in Rome were continuing to operate within the larger Jewish community while including non-Jews, representing the other nations, as equal members of God's people. 'For Paul,' Nanos writes, 'this communal gathering thereby exemplifies the arrival of the end of the ages, when…the wolf will graze with, rather than devour, the lamb (Isa 65.25).'[7]

What is intriguing about this claim is that Paul (as well as other New Testament writers) nowhere *explicitly* borrows Isa 65.25 (or the similar 2.4 or 11.6) or other go-to images of the age of *shalom*, such as swords being turned into ploughshares, or even the precise phrase 'Prince of Peace.' Nonetheless, Nanos is right that Paul saw the existence of Jews and Gentiles together, not only as the eschatological ingathering of the nations to worship YHWH, but also as a fundamental and substantive sign that the eschatological age of *shalom* has arrived in Jesus the Messiah.

> **Paul connected the peace offered in Jesus the Messiah with the shalom texts of Isaiah**

There is ample evidence that Paul did connect the peace offered in Jesus the Messiah with the *shalom* texts and motifs of Isaiah 2, 11, 65, and similar passages in Isaiah. Like other Second Temple writers, Paul was drawn to such texts, as evidenced in quotations and allusions, but—also like many Second Temple writers—he did not utilize some of the images we might have expected.[8]

Within the Scriptures of Israel, the coming age, when a covenant of peace will be established, is described most frequently and fully in Isaiah. There are several elements that emerge from these texts taken as a cluster, forming a literary composite, a *shalom*-collage, so to speak—or perhaps, in addition, a kind of *shalom*-narrative in the making.[9] We can construct this narrative-collage of peace primarily from parts of Isaiah 2, 9, 11, 32, 52, 54, 55, 60, 61 and 65, without claiming that the prophet Isaiah, the book's compiler(s), or Paul had such a narrative-collage explicitly in mind. Rather, it may be that someone like Paul, who was intimately familiar with this prophetic book and, it appears, with these thematically connected texts, would naturally allude to their features at various junctures, even as he just as naturally reinterpreted them in light of the actual Messianic event. As Steve Moyise has put it, Paul works within an 'overall [Isaiah] narrative framework.'[10]

Among the several texts from Isaiah that contribute to this *shalom*-collage, one of the most important, quoted or echoed in many Second Temple Jewish writers (including Paul, as we will see), is Isaiah 11, which describes a 'shoot… from the stump of Jesse' who, by God's Spirit, will bring about righteousness and equity, especially for the poor (11.1–5). As a result, 'The wolf shall live with the lamb,' '[T]he nursing child shall play over the hole of the asp,' and '[T]hey will not hurt or destroy on all my holy mountain' (11.6–9). Moreover, the people of God will be reunited, and the mutual jealousy and hostility dividing Ephraim and Judah will cease (11.13).

A few other texts are worthy of special note, including Isa 2.2–4: 'The nations shall stream' to 'the mountain of the Lord,' and when the Lord judges 'between the nations,' they shall 'beat their swords into plowshares, and their spears into pruning hooks; nation shall not lift up sword against nation, neither shall they learn war any more.' And of course there is Isaiah 9, which predicts the arrival of a 'Prince of Peace' (9.6).

Isaiah predicts the arrival of a 'Prince of Peace'

Similar is Isaiah 32, with its promise that 'a king will reign in righteousness, and princes will rule with justice' so that the 'effect of righteousness will be peace, and the result of righteousness, quietness and trust forever' and '[M]y people will abide in a peaceful habitation, in secure dwellings, and in quiet resting places' (Isa 32.1, 17–18).

Just prior to the famous text of Isaiah 53, the prophet announces, 'How beautiful upon the mountains are the feet of the messenger who announces peace, who brings good news, who announces salvation, who says to Zion, "Your God reigns"' and 'all the ends of the earth shall see the salvation of our God' (Isa 52.7, 10). And just after chapter 53, God promises that 'My steadfast love shall not depart from you, and my covenant of peace shall not be removed' (54.10).

In the latter part of Isaiah, the Lord promises to 'appoint Peace as your overseer and Righteousness as your taskmaster' so that '[v]iolence shall no more be heard in your land, devastation or destruction within your borders' (Isa 60.17b–18). The 'everlasting covenant' (61.8) will be a time of liberation (61.1) and justice (61.8). And the book's final vision, of 'new heavens and a new earth' (65.17), will mean the reign of joy and the end of calamity and death (65.18–24) as the promise of Isaiah 2 is echoed in a new idiom: 'The wolf and the lamb shall feed together, the lion shall eat straw like the ox; but the serpent—its food shall be dust! They shall not hurt or destroy on all my holy mountain, says the Lord' (Isa 65.25).

This *shalom* narrative-collage and vision are most fully expressed in the book of Isaiah, but they can also be found in visionary texts elsewhere in the Scriptures of Israel, sometimes in the poetry of the psalms (some of which are used by Paul and noted below), sometimes in the voice of another prophet, especially Ezekiel. As quoted earlier, Ezek 34.25 speaks of a 'covenant of peace' that will mean unity, security, and abundance. Indeed, all of the peace themes we have identified from Isaiah (except the explicit language of 'good news' and perhaps the inclusion of the Gentiles) are substantively present in Ezek 34.22–31 and 37.21–28, where 'a covenant of peace' also appears (37.26).

The elements found in these various visions in Isaiah and Ezekiel include at least the following:

- Peace as good news (Isa 52.7; *cf* 61.1)

- Peace as the peaceful reign of God and / or God's son / Davidic king / delegate (*eg* Isa 9.6–7; 11.1, 10; 32.1; 52.7; Ezek 34.23–24; 37.22, 24a, 25, 26)

- Peace as a reconciled covenant relationship with Israel's loving God (Isa 54.10; Ezek 34.24, 30–31; 37.23b, 26)[11]

- Peace as deliverance from and / or the defeat of Israel's enemies (Isa 9.4–5; 11.4b, 14–16; Ezek 34.27)

- Peace as the redemption / restoration of Israel (*eg* Isa 9.2–3; 11.10–13, 16; 52.9; 65.18; Ezek 34.22–23; 37.21, 25) and the inclusion of the Gentiles / nations / ends of the earth in God's salvation (*eg* Isa 2.2–3; 9.1–2; 52.10)

- Peace as the reconciliation of natural enemies / those who have been divided, and resulting harmony (Isa 11.6–9, 13; 65.25; Ezek 34.22–23; 37.22, 24a)

- Peace as the absence of violence (*eg* Isa 2.4; 11.9; 60.18; 65.25; *cf* 59.6–8; Ezek 34.28)

- Peace as inclusive of righteousness and justice (*eg* Isa 2.4a; 9.7; 11.3b–4a, 5; 32.1, 16–17; 60.17; *cf* 59.6–8; 61.1–11; Ezek 37.23a, 24b)

- Peace as security / safety (*eg* Isa 11.6–9; 32.18; 54.12; 65.19b–23, 25; Ezek 34.25, 28; 37.26)

- Peace as enabled by God / God's Spirit and inclusive of God's presence (*eg* Isa 11.2; 32.15; 52.8; Ezek 34.24–25; 37.26–28)

- Peace as joyful flourishing and abundance, salvation, and even a new creation (*eg* Isa 52.8; 55.12–13; 60.18; 65.17–18, 21–24; Ezek 34.26–27, 29; 37.25–26)

In sum, this new era anticipated by the prophetic tradition of Isaiah and Ezekiel will be an age of peace, indeed a 'covenant of peace.' In more typically Pauline language, they promise a 'gospel of peace' (Eph 6.15; compare Isa 52.7).

6 Paul and Luke Join the Isaiah–Ezekiel Concert

A careful comparison of texts from Isaiah and Ezekiel demonstrates that each of the eleven elements of peace from these two prophetic books, identified above, appears in the Pauline corpus, scattered throughout but also sometimes clustered, in a way rather similar to what we find in the prophets themselves. The themes appear as well in the Gospel of Luke and in Acts. The following table (with NRSV text) sets these Isaiah/Ezekiel themes and Pauline/Lukan parallels out in relationship to one another. (Space does not permit the citation of all relevant texts.)[12]

'The Covenant of Peace': Parallel Peace Texts in Isaiah/Ezekiel and Paul/Luke

Theme from Isaiah/ Ezekiel Texts	Parallel Pauline and Lukan Texts
1. Peace as good news	• Eph 6.15 (the gospel of peace); *cf* Rom 10.15 (good news) • Luke 2.10, 14 ('Good news of great joy…on earth peace.') • Acts 10.36 ('Preaching [the good news of peace] by Jesus Christ.')
2. Peace as the peaceful reign of God and/or God's son/Davidic king/ delegate	• Rom 14.17 ('The kingdom of God is…righteousness [or justice] and peace and joy in the Holy Spirit.') • Rom 15.33; 16.20; 1 Cor 1.7, 15; 14.33; 2 Cor 13.11; Phil 4.9; 1 Thess 5.23 (God of peace, etc) • Col 3.15 ('And let the peace of Christ rule in your hearts, to which indeed you were called.') • 2 Thess 3.16 ('Now may the Lord of peace himself give you peace at all times in all ways.') • Luke 1.31–33, 69 ('The Lord God will give to him the throne of his ancestor David, of his kingdom there will be no end.') • Luke 2.11 ('To you is born this day in the city of David a Savior, who is the Messiah, the Lord.') • Luke 18.38–39; 20.41–44 (Son of David); *cf* Acts 13.32–37 • Acts 8.12 (good news about the kingdom of God and the name of Jesus Christ)

3. Peace as a reconciled covenant relationship with Israel's loving God	• Rom 5.1–11 ('Peace with God through our Lord Jesus Christ…While we were enemies, we were reconciled to God…') • Eph 2.17–18 ('So he came and proclaimed peace to you who were far off and peace to those who were near'); *cf* Col 1.20–22 • *cf* 2 Cor 5.18–21 (in Christ God was reconciling the world to himself) • Luke 1.16–17 ('He [John] will turn many of the people of Israel to the Lord their God.') • Luke 1.76–79 ('You [John] will go before the Lord to prepare his ways, to give knowledge of salvation to his people by the forgiveness of their sins…The dawn from on high will break upon us…to guide our feet into the way of peace.') • Luke 7.50; 8.48 (your faith has saved you/made you well; 'Go in peace.') • Acts 2.38 ('Repent, and be baptized every one of you in the name of Jesus Christ so that your sins may be forgiven.')
4. Peace as deliverance from and/or the defeat of Israel's enemies	• Rom 16.20 ('The God of peace will shortly crush Satan under your feet.') • *cf* 1 Cor 15.24–27, 54–57 (the last enemy to be destroyed is death.) • *cf* Col 2.13–15 ('God…forgave us all our trespasses, erasing the record that stood against us with its legal demands. He set this aside, nailing it to the cross.') • *cf* 2 Cor 10.1–6; 1 Thess 5.8, 15; Eph 6.10–18 (believers' participation in spiritual battles) • Luke 1.71, 74 ('That we would be saved from our enemies and from the hand of all who hate us…that we, being rescued from the hands of our enemies, might serve him without fear.') • Luke 10.17–19 ('"Lord, in your name even the demons submit to us!" He [Jesus] said to them, "I watched Satan fall from heaven like a flash of lightning."') • *cf* Acts 9.23–25; 12.11 (deliverance of Saul and Peter from enemies)

| 5. Peace as the redemption/restoration of Israel

and

the inclusion of the Gentiles/nations/ends of the earth in God's salvation | • Gal 6.15–16 ('As for those who will follow this rule [about new creation not circumcision]—peace be upon them, and mercy, and upon the Israel of God.')

• Eph 2.14–17 ('For he is our peace…he has made both groups into one and has broken down the dividing wall…that he might create in himself one new humanity…thus making peace, and might reconcile both groups to God in one body through the cross…So he came and proclaimed peace…')

• Rom 14.1—15.13 ('May the God of hope fill you with all joy and peace in believing.' [15.13])

• *cf* Rom 9–11 (*eg* 11.15: 'For if their rejection is the reconciliation of the world, what will their acceptance be but life from the dead!')

• Luke 1.54–55, 68 ('He has helped his servant…He has looked favourably on his people and redeemed them.')

• Luke 2.25, 29–32 ('Master, now you are dismissing your servant in peace, my eyes have seen your salvation, a light for revelation to the Gentiles and for glory to your people Israel.')

• *cf* Luke 7.1–17 (healing of a Gentile centurion's slave, raising of a Jewish woman's son from the dead)

• Acts 11.17–18 ('"If then God gave them [the Gentiles] the same gift that he gave us when we believed in the Lord Jesus Christ, who was I that I could hinder God?"') |
| 6. Peace as the reconciliation of natural enemies/those who have been divided, and resulting harmony | • Rom 12.18 (live peaceably with all); *cf* 14.19; 2 Cor 13.11; 1 Thess 5.13, 15

• Eph 2.14–16 (see above, under no 5)

• Eph 4.2–3 ('…making every effort to maintain the unity of the Spirit in the bond of peace.')

• Eph 6.23 (peace be to the whole community)

• Col 1.20 ('…and through him God was pleased to reconcile to himself all things…by making peace through the blood of his cross.')

• Col 3.15 ('And let the peace of Christ rule in your hearts, to which indeed you were called in the one body.'); *cf* Gal 5.20

• *cf* Phile 15–16 ('No longer as a slave but more than a slave, a beloved brother')

• Luke 12.57–59 ('"Thus, when you go with your accuser before a magistrate, on the way make an effort to settle the case."')

• Acts 10 (the acceptance of Cornelius and the Gentiles/ Romans; 10.36 = 'peace by Jesus Christ')

• Acts 15.1–35 (after the Jerusalem meeting acknowledges no distinction between them [Gentiles] and us [15.9], Judas and Silas are 'sent off in peace' [15.33]) |

7. Peace as the absence of violence	<ul><li>1 Thess 5.15 ('See that none of you repays evil for evil.')</li><li>Rom 12.14–21 ('Bless those who persecute you; bless and do not curse them…Do not repay anyone evil for evil…Beloved, never avenge yourselves.')</li><li>*cf* Rom 3.13–17 ('…Their feet are swift to shed blood…and the way of peace they have not known.')</li><li>Luke 6.27–29, 35 ('Love your enemies, do good to those who hate you, bless those who curse you, pray for those who abuse you. If anyone strikes you on the cheek, offer the other also.')</li><li>Luke 9.54b–55 ('"Lord, do you want us to command fire to come down from heaven and consume them?" But he turned and rebuked them.'); *cf* 22.36–38, 49–51</li><li>Luke 23.34 ('Father, forgive them; for they do not know what they are doing.')</li><li>Acts 7.60 ('Lord, do not hold this sin against them.')</li><li>Acts 9.31 (peace and church growth)</li></ul>
8. Peace as inclusive of righteousness and justice	<ul><li>Rom 5.1 ('…justified by faith…peace with God.')</li><li>Rom 12.17, 21 (see above, under no 7)</li><li>Rom 14.16–19 ('The kingdom of God is…righteousness [or justice] and peace and joy…Let us then pursue what makes for peace and for mutual upbuilding.')</li><li>1 Thess 5.15 (see above, under no 7)</li><li>2 Tim 2.22 ('Pursue righteousness, faith, love, and peace.')</li><li>*cf* Rom 3.13–17 ('Their feet are swift to shed blood…and the way of peace they have not known.')</li><li>*cf* 2 Cor 5.21 ('For our sake he made him to be sin who knew no sin, so that in him we might become the righteousness of God.')</li><li>Luke 1.17 ('He [John] will go before him, to turn the hearts of parents to their children, and the disobedient to the wisdom of the righteous.')</li><li>Luke 1.74–75 ('…that we…might serve him without fear, in holiness and righteousness before him all our days.')</li></ul>
9. Peace as security/ safety	<ul><li>1 Cor 16.11 ('Send him on his way in peace.')</li><li>Phil 4.7 ('And the peace of God, which surpasses all understanding, will guard your hearts and your minds in Christ Jesus.')</li><li>1 Thess 5.3 ('When they say, "There is peace and security."')</li><li>Luke 1.74 ('…that we, being rescued from the hands of our enemies, might serve him without fear.')</li><li>Luke 10.19 ('I have given you authority to tread on snakes and scorpions, and over all the power of the enemy; and nothing will hurt you.')</li><li>Acts 9.31 (peace and church growth)</li></ul>

10. Peace as enabled by God/God's Spirit and inclusive of God's presence	• Benedictions: peace from God/Christ; the God of peace (Rom 1.7; 15.13, 33; 1 Cor 1.3; 2 Cor 1.2; 13.11; Gal 6.16; 2 Thess 3.16; etc)
	• Rom 8.6 ('…to set the mind on the Spirit is life and peace.')
	• Rom 14.17 ('The kingdom of God is…joy in the Holy Spirit.')
	• Gal 5.22 ('The fruit of the Spirit is love, joy, peace.')
	• Eph 4.2–3 ('…making every effort to maintain the unity of the Spirit in the bond of peace.')
	• Phil 4.7–9 ('And the peace of God, which surpasses all understanding, will guard your hearts and your minds in Christ Jesus…and the God of peace will be with you.')
	• Luke 4.18–19 ('"The Spirit of the Lord is upon me, because he has anointed me to bring good news to the poor…to proclaim release…to let the oppressed go free…"')
	• Acts 2.1–18 ('I will pour out my Spirit upon all flesh'); *cf* Acts 2.38–39
11. Peace as joyful flourishing and abundance, salvation, and even a new creation	• Rom 2.10 ('…glory and honour and peace for everyone who does good.')
	• Rom 8.6 ('to set the mind on the Spirit is life and peace')
	• Rom 14.17 ('The kingdom of God is…joy in the Holy Spirit.')
	• Rom 15.13 ('May the God of hope fill you with all joy and peace…')
	• Gal 6.15–16 ('…a new creation is everything! As for those who will follow this rule—peace be upon them…')
	• Phil 4.4–7 (Rejoice in the Lord…rejoice. Do not worry…but… let your requests be made known to God. And the peace of God…will guard your hearts and your minds in Christ Jesus.')
	• Col 1.20 ('…and through him God was pleased to reconcile to himself all things, whether on earth or in heaven, by making peace through the blood of his cross.')
	• *cf* 2 Cor 5.17 ('So if anyone is in Christ, there is a new creation.')
	• Luke 2.10 ('…good news of great joy for all the people.'); *cf* 1.41, 44
	• Luke 10.17 ('The seventy returned with joy, saying, "Lord, in your name even the demons submit to us!"')
	• Luke 15.7, 10 ('joy' in heaven/the presence of the angels of God over one sinner who repents)
	• Acts 8.7–8 ('…unclean spirits, crying with loud shrieks, came out of many who were possessed; and many others who were paralyzed or lame were cured. So there was great joy in that city.')

We cannot consider all of these many texts, but we turn now to some interpretive comments about both Paul and Luke.

The Covenant of Peace in Paul

I am proposing that Paul himself understood that the 'peace of God/Christ/ the Messiah' (Phil 4.7; Col 3.15) about which he spoke was in fact the peace promised by Isaiah (and Ezekiel) in the texts from which we have drawn our narrative-collage, and this despite the absence of certain key images. All of the prophetic themes identified above are transformed in the Pauline corpus as they are reworked in light of the reality of the crucified and resurrected Jesus as Messiah.[13]

The question naturally arises, 'Did Paul himself know what he was doing?' He certainly does not provide us with an in-depth exegesis of any of Isaiah's peace passages. Indeed, there are probably only three marked citations of relevant Isaiah texts, so we are dealing largely with allusions and echoes.[14] And in one instance—when Paul explicitly cites Isa 52.7, about good news of peace and salvation (Rom 10.15)—he omits the reference to peace:

> And how are they to proclaim him unless they are sent? As it is written, 'How beautiful are the feet of those who bring good news!' (Rom 10.15, omitting 'the messenger who announces peace')

Paul also omits the references to salvation and to the reign of God in Isa 52.7, not because he discounts either of those realities—or the reality of peace—but because his immediate focus in the context of Romans 10 is the word 'gospel/ good news' (Rom 10.16) and the corollary imperative to mission symbolized by 'feet.'

More explicit evidence that Paul does find the promised peace of Isaiah fulfilled in Jesus comes in another marked citation. In Rom 15.12, as Paul concludes his admonition to, and celebration of, unity among Gentiles and Jews in Messiah Jesus within the Roman house churches, he quotes Isa 11.10 in abbreviated form:

> Again Isaiah says, 'The root of Jesse shall come, the one who rises to rule the Gentiles; in him the Gentiles shall hope.'

The LXX of Isa 11.10 actually reads 'and there shall be *on that day* the root of Jesse…' Paul's omission of the italicized phrase, referring back to the poetic prophecy of vv 1–9, likely occurs because Paul believes the hoped-for coming day is no longer future but present; the root of Jesse, the hope of the nations, has inaugurated that which vv 1–9 anticipate, a time of righteousness, faithfulness, peace, and knowledge of YHWH. These are the traits of the messianic age. In 11.10–11 Isaiah extends these benefits beyond Israel to the Gentiles; he globalizes the messianic peace.

Paul's omission of 'in that day' indicates that he has read the verse he cites in context. For him, the inclusion of the Gentiles is an essential part of the peace of God that the Messiah Jesus has inaugurated. In Rom 15.9–13, Paul is not merely creating a catena of texts testifying to the inclusion of the Gentiles, or nations, in God's salvation. He is telling his audience that the inclusion of the nations is part of the great divine, messianic peace initiative to bring together Israel and non-Israel, to reconcile and unite those who are at odds in one way or another. The inclusion of the Gentiles also means the reconciliation of the Gentiles with Jews and with one another. It is this conviction that drives Rom 15.7–13, the letter's peroration, with the opening admonition to 'Welcome one another, therefore, just as Christ has welcomed you, for the glory of God' (15.7), as well as the closing benediction, 'May the God of hope fill you with all joy and peace in believing, so that you may abound in hope by the power of the Holy Spirit' (15.13)—both rooted in the reality that the peacemaking Messiah has come and is still here in the powerful, peaceable presence of the Spirit.

Indeed, the previous passage (Rom 15.1–6) indicates that the Messiah's cruciform love—which is of course also the reconciling love of God (Rom. 5.5, 8; 8.28, 39; 2 Cor 5.14, 21)—is both the source and the shape of people's reconciliation with God and with one another, so that the purpose of human existence may come to fruition:

> May the God of steadfastness and encouragement grant you to live in harmony with one another, in accordance with Christ Jesus, so that together you may with one voice glorify the God and Father of our Lord Jesus Christ. (Rom 15.5–6)

Themes and visions of peace similar to those of Isaiah may of course be found elsewhere in the Bible. One that resonates well with the Isaianic texts, and with Paul, is Psalm 85 (LXX 84), which includes the following lines:

> Will you not revive us again, so that your people may rejoice in you?
>
> Show us your steadfast love, O Lord, and grant us your salvation.

Paul echoes and summarizes this psalm in Rom 14.17 as a kind of synopsis of his convictions about the peace of God in Christ: 'For the kingdom of God is not food and drink but righteousness and peace (*dikaiosynē kai eirēnē*) and joy in the Holy Spirit.' This, in turn, is not far from being a summary of Rom 5.1–11, in which Paul claims that in the crucified and resurrected Messiah God has lovingly offered humanity righteousness/justice and peace/reconciliation, known now experientially by the presence of the Spirit: 'Therefore, since we are justified (*dikaiōthentes*) by faith, we have peace (*eirēnēn*) with God through our Lord Jesus Christ.' Indeed, Isaiah had written, 'The effect of righteousness (*dikaiosynēs*) will be peace (*eirēnē*)' (Isa 32.17). The phrase 'peace and righteousness [or justice]' is frequently shorthand for the eschatological or messianic age both in Israel's Scriptures—including Isaiah specifically—and in some Second Temple texts.[15] Paul both knows this slogan and develops it, as Rom 5.1, Rom 14.17, and several other texts make clear.

For Paul, then, Jesus is indeed the Prince of Peace, the one through whom God has made and is making the promised messianic *shalom*, the covenant of *shalom*, reality.

Of course, as all interpreters of Paul recognize, this reality is not yet here in its fullness. Paul, of all people, is painfully aware of this truth, as he experiences anxiety, strife, and even violence in his own life (see, for example, 2 Cor 11.22–30)—quite the opposite of security and reconciliation. Paradoxically, Paul can associate even this aspect of believing existence with the peace of Christ. He writes to the Philippians as follows:

The phrase 'labour in vain' (*eis kenon ekopiasa*) appears to be based on Isa 65.23, 'They shall not labour in vain [LXX *ou kopiasousin eis kenon*] or bear children for calamity; for they shall be offspring blessed by the Lord—and their descendants as well,' part of the glorious vision of the coming new creation. Paul, who knows the new creation has begun, understands in light of the narrative of Jesus that the new creation does not come without a price (2 Cor 5.17; Gal 6.15). His suffering will have been worth the cost if his churches remain faithful to the gospel, with the result that he can then know that his work of proclaiming the good news of reconciliation and new creation was not in vain. Even in the present struggles, however, those in the Messiah can know the peace of the Messiah, as Paul reminds the Philippians (Phil 4.7, 9).

It should come as no surprise, then, that Paul repeatedly calls the church that has *received* God's peace to *practise* God's peace (*eg* Rom 12.18; 14.19; 1 Cor 7.15; 16.11; 2 Cor 13.11; Gal 5.22; Eph 4.3; Col 3.15; 1 Thess 5.13; 2 Tim 2.22).

To summarize: for Paul, Jesus is the prophetically promised Prince of Peace, the Lord of peace, who inaugurates the age and the covenant of peace and calls the church to peace. The echoes we have considered were available to Paul; they recur; cohere and have sufficient volume to be heard, and they are both historically plausible and satisfying.[16]

The Covenant of Peace in Luke

As noted above, the word 'peace' does not occur frequently in Luke-Acts. Nevertheless, peace is critical to the narrative; it is announced at highly significant moments, and it is woven into the very fabric of Luke's two-volume work, especially the Gospel of Luke. Willard Swartley rightly claims that the way Luke uses the vocabulary of peace indicates that peace 'expresses the very heart of the gospel.'[17] Like Paul, Luke is quite fond of Isaiah, and the *shalom*—God's peace and justice—promised in the Book of Isaiah and elsewhere is one of several complementary prophetic themes that work together to convey Luke's understanding of the salvation wrought by God through Jesus and in the power of the Spirit. We look, therefore, at the narrative as a whole.

The word 'peace' makes its first appearance in the Benedictus, which ends on the word 'peace'; it is the culmination of Zechariah's hope/prophecy—the reality that his son John (the Baptist) will prepare and that the Messiah will bring (Luke 1.68–79). God will mercifully guide the people out of the 'shadow of death' into 'the way of peace' (1.79), meaning deliverance from enemies, forgiveness and salvation, and service to God in security.

At several points, these words echo Mary's Magnificat (1.46–55), suggesting that the way of peace that the Messiah brings will, paradoxically, not be so peaceful—at least not in the sense of calm (see 12.51). It will involve reversal of the status quo (so especially 1.52–53) and defeat of enemies, even if Luke later makes it clear that Jesus the Messiah will not deal with enemies violently, as certain other Second Temple Jews would have wanted to do.

Furthermore, both the Magnificat and the Benedictus refer to God's covenantal promise to Abraham (1.54–55, 72–73), suggesting that what is about to happen in the Messiah Jesus is the renewal of the covenant. Although neither poetic text uses the language of 'new' covenant, Luke is making it clear that what is about to transpire is covenantal, and when Jesus announces at the Last Supper that his death is effecting the 'new covenant in my blood' (22.20), we are brought back to these opening announcements.

Following the words of Zechariah, we have almost immediately the words of the heavenly host at the birth of the 'dawn from on high' (1.78; compare Isa 9.2; 60.1–2), their burst of praise confirming the promise of Zechariah: '"Glory to God in the highest heaven, and on earth peace among those whom he favours!"' (2.14). In implicit but clear contrast to Caesar Augustus, Lord and Messiah Jesus, the Son of David and Son of the Most High God, is the bringer of God's peace on those who are the recipients of divine benefactions.[18] By implication, it is Jesus, not Caesar, who is Isaiah's 'Prince of Peace' (Isa 9.6) and lord of peace (60.17b).

The truth of these promises is quickly reconfirmed in the praise of Simeon as he holds the infant saviour: '"Master, now you are dismissing your servant in peace, according to your word; for my eyes have seen your salvation…"' (2.29–31), an echo of Isa 52.7–10 and its promise of salvation and peace. The covenant of peace has arrived.

These first three peace texts in Luke—the promise of imminent peace to be brought by the Messiah (1.79), the inauguration of peace in the birth of the Messiah (2.14), and the confession of Simeon (2.29–30)—are programmatic for Luke's gospel and his entire theological project. They tell us what the ministry of the Messiah consists of: inaugurating the age of peace and thereby creating a community, a people, of *shalom*—a covenant community that experiences and practises God's peace and justice. Indeed, these initial texts establish the context for the additional indications of Jesus' ministry that emerge in the gospel: Jesus' being about his Father's business (1.49), baptizing with the Holy Spirit (3.15–17), announcing the good news of liberation for the oppressed in fulfilment of Isaiah's promise of *shalom* (4.14–21), bringing God's healing and delivering power to all in need of liberation from oppression (4.31–44 and afterwards), and teaching the way of peace (*eg* 6.20–49). These are cardinal aspects of the messianic reign of *shalom* and the 'everlasting covenant' described in Isaiah 61.

If the Gospel of Luke begins on a repeated note of peace, it also culminates on such a note. When Jesus, who has 'set his face to go to Jerusalem' (9.51) less than halfway through the narrative, arrives in Jerusalem, where he is to die, he is greeted by a 'multitude of the disciples' (19.37) saying, '"Blessed is the king who comes in the name of the Lord! Peace in heaven, and glory in the highest heaven!"' (19.38). This clear echo of the angels in 2.14 (and words not found in Mark or Matthew) establishes a literary *inclusio* and a theological claim: the good news of peace Jesus was born to bring is being brought to a new level, a fuller conclusion, with his imminent death.

Moreover, as Luke narrates Jesus' trip to Jerusalem and his 'exodus'/death there (9.31), he makes it clear that this death is Jesus'—and God's—act of peacemaking as well as a summons to discipleship in the form of sharing in that death. Luke gives voice to this costly dimension of discipleship both by using the traditional summonses to discipleship he takes from Mark's passion predictions and by including one at the Last Supper (22.23–27). Luke also places certain parts of the sermonic material that is similar to Matthew 5–7 in the context of the journey to Jerusalem (*eg* the Lord's Prayer, with its challenge to forgiveness: 11.2–4).

The new community is defined by the road to Jerusalem and all that it entails; if the community of the new covenant (the disciples) is so defined, then also the Lord of the new covenant is defined by how and why he goes to Jerusalem. He goes in peace, and he instructs the disciples to follow. When one of the disciples cuts off the ear of the high priest's slave, there is Jesus rejecting violence (22.51a) and making *shalom*, bringing the healing that has characterized his Isaianic ministry to the party of his enemies (22.51b). Luke alone records this healing. It is not merely an enacted parable of peacemaking but an instantiation of the kind of peaceful new covenant his death brings about: 'They shall not hurt or destroy' (Isa 65.25).

Jesus' way of dying demonstrates, and his death effects, the forgiveness of sins promised by Zechariah (Luke 1.77). The peacemaking dimension of the Messiah's death is captured perhaps most poignantly in the first words Jesus speaks from the cross: '"Father, forgive them; for they do not know what they are doing"' (23.34a). This merciful, gracious pronouncement is significant because it embodies, at the ultimate point of testing and temptation to betray one's one most deeply held convictions, Jesus' teaching about enemy-love and his practice of forgiveness throughout his ministry. Furthermore, we must assume that for Luke the 'them' includes Jewish leaders as well as Roman soldiers and officials, ironically furthering the theme of the gospel's being for both Jews and Gentiles. The words of Jesus are equally important, moreover, as a prayer to the Father, for Jesus the Prophet-Messiah-Son has come into the world, and has come to this unjust place on earth, precisely to bring God's *shalom*, God's peace and justice, to the earth.

All of this is why Peter, in Acts 10.36, can allude to Isaiah 52.7 and 61.1 and rightly summarize God's activity in Jesus as 'preaching the good news of peace by Jesus Christ' (my translation). Here and throughout Acts, preaching the good news (using the verb *euangelizomai*) is expressed in various ways: preaching the Messiah, Jesus (5.42); preaching the kingdom of God and the name of Jesus (8.12); preaching the Lord Jesus (Acts 11.20); preaching God's promises fulfilled in Jesus' resurrection (Acts 13.32). These are obviously not different gospels but one gospel, which can be called first and foremost, according to Luke's narrative, the gospel of peace.

It therefore makes sense for us to look at Luke-Acts as a narrative of the arrival of the prophetically promised covenant of peace. Not only does the covenant of peace arrive in Jesus, but this covenant of peace is the will and activity of God the Father, it is empowered by the Spirit, and it takes shape not only in the ministry of Jesus, but also in the life of his disciples and in the life of the church as narrated in Acts.

9

Conclusion

We have seen that for Paul and Luke, two of the New Testament's chief theologians, the prophetically promised era of peace, the covenant of peace, has arrived in the Messiah Jesus, and that this is a significant part of the theological project of each author. We have looked at specific texts from the writings of Paul and Luke that use the word 'peace' and/or contain echoes of the principal themes about peace drawn from the prophets Isaiah and Ezekiel.

Much more could be said, especially about Jesus' death as God's act of peacemaking, and about the ecclesial practice of peace and peacemaking that flow from the life and death of Jesus. But the main point is abundantly clear: according to the witness of Paul and Luke, peace is not a supplement to New Testament theology and spirituality; it is at the very centre.

Bibliography for Further Study

Paul Borgmann, *The Way According to Luke: Hearing the Whole Story of Luke-Acts* (Grand Rapids, MI: Eerdmans, 2006).

Laura L Brenneman and Brad D Schantz (eds), *Struggles for Shalom* (Eugene, OR: Pickwick, 2014).

Pieter G R De Villiers, 'Peace in Luke and Acts: A Perspective on Biblical Spirituality.' *Acta Patristica et Byzantina* 19 (2008): pp 110–34.

Pieter G R De Villiers, 'Peace in the Pauline Letters: A Perspective on Biblical Spirituality,' *Neotestamentica* 43 (2009): pp 1–26.

Jeremy Gabrielson, *Paul's Non-Violent Gospel: The Theological Politics of Peace in Paul's Life and Letters* (Eugene, OR: Pickwick, 2013).

Michael J Gorman, *Becoming the Gospel: Paul, Participation, and Mission* (Grand Rapids, MI: Eerdmans, 2015). See especially chapters five and six.

Michael J Gorman, *The Death of the Messiah and the Birth of the New Covenant: A (Not So) New Model of the Atonement* (Eugene, OR: Cascade, 2014). See especially chapters six and seven.

Darrell D Hannah, 'Isaiah within Judaism of the Second Temple Period,' In *Isaiah in the New Testament*, edited by Steve Moyise and Maarten J J Menken (London: T and T Clark, 2005) pp 7–34.

Richard B Hays, *Echoes of Scripture in the Letters of Paul* (New Haven, CT: Yale University Press, 1989).

John Kilgallen, '"Peace" in the Gospel of Luke and Acts of the Apostles,' *Studia Missionalia* 38 (1989): pp 55–79.

Steve Moyise, *Evoking Scripture: Seeing the Old Testament in the New* (London: T and T Clark, 2008).

Mark D Nanos, 'To the Churches within the Synagogues of Rome,' in Jerry L Sumney (ed), *Reading Paul's Letter to the Romans* (Atlanta: Society of Biblical Literature, 2012) pp 11–28.

Willard M Swartley, *Covenant of Peace: The Missing Peace in New Testament Theology and Ethics* (Grand Rapids, MI: Eerdmans, 2006).

J Ross Wagner, *Heralds of the Good News: Isaiah and Paul in Concert in the Letter to the Romans* (Leiden: Brill, 2003).

Klaus Wengst (trans John Bowden), *Pax Romana and the Peace of Jesus Christ* (Philadelphia, PA: Fortress, 1987).

N T Wright, *Paul and the Faithfulness of God* (London: SPCK/Minneapolis, MN: Fortress, 2013).

Notes

1 See also Num 25.12–13; Mal 2.4–5; Sir 45.24.

2 Udo Schnelle, *Apostle Paul: His Life and Theology*, trans M Eugene Boring (Grand Rapids, MI: Baker Academic, 2005). For peace as 'conventional,' see p 187.

3 François Bovon, *Luke the Theologian* (Waco, TX: Baylor University Press, 2006) p 223 (source of the quotation); p 302.

4 Darrell L Bock, *A Theology of Luke and Acts: God's Promised Program, Realized for All Nations* (Grand Rapids, MI: Zondervan, 2012) p 271.

5 Paul Borgmann, *The Way According to Luke: Hearing the Whole Story of Luke-Acts* (Grand Rapids, MI: Eerdmans, 2006) p x.

6 I allude to Ross Wagner's brilliant book on Paul's use of Isaiah, *Heralds of the Good News*.

7 Mark D Nanos, 'To the Churches within the Synagogues of Rome,' in Jerry L Sumney (ed), *Reading Paul's Letter to the Romans* (Atlanta: Society of Biblical Literature, 2012) p 27.

8 For a brief but helpful overview of the use of Isaiah in Second Temple literature, see Darrell D Hannah, 'Isaiah within Judaism of the Second Temple Period,' in Steve Moyise and Maarten J J Menken (eds), *Isaiah in the New Testament* (London: T and T Clark, 2005) pp 7–34.

9 See J Ross Wagner, *Heralds of the Good News: Isaiah and Paul in Concert in the Letter to the Romans* (Leiden: Brill, 2003) for the implicit soteriological narrative in the Book of Isaiah.

10 Steve Moyise, *Evoking Scripture: Seeing the Old Testament in the New* (London: T and T Clark, 2008) p 49, summarizing his discussion on pp 33–48.

11 For additional promises of a future covenant, see Isa 42.6–7; 49.8; 55.1–5; 59.21; and 61.8.

12 All texts from Paul cited in the list below contain the noun *eirēnē* (or the verb *eirēneuō*) or *eirēnopoieō* except those preceded by '*cf*' (Many of the latter contain *katalassō* [reconcile], etc). Many of the texts from Luke are deliberately taken from the programmatic statements early in the gospel. Unlike the Pauline texts, however, the word 'peace' does not appear in every text cited; Luke's vocabulary of *shalom* is larger than the word 'peace.'

13 It is also important to note two of the Isaianic themes (4 and 5 above) that receive particularly radical reinterpretation in Paul. Unlike some of the Dead Sea Scrolls and the Psalms of Solomon, Paul has no interest in the literal destruction of human enemies. And unlike Isaiah himself, Paul does not focus on the restoration of Israel as a nation *per se* or on Jerusalem as a city, and he does not pick up on the prophetic notion of the subjugation of the Gentiles as part of the future peace (eg Isaiah 60).

14 The marked citations are Rom 3.17 = Isa 59.8; Rom 10.15 = Isa 52.7; Rom 15.12 = Isa 11.10.

15 For example, Isa 32.16; 60.17. See also, for example, Test Judah 24.1.

16 I refer to the main criteria proposed by Richard Hays (*Echoes of Scripture*, pp 29–32) for discerning the presence of scriptural echoes.

17 Willard M Swartley, *Covenant of Peace: The Missing Peace in New Testament Theology and Ethics* (Grand Rapids, MI: Eerdmans, 2006) p 130.

18 Contrast the famous calendar inscription of 9 BCE in Priene and elsewhere in the province of Asia that honours Caesar Augustus as the one 'whom virtue has filled for the benefit of humankind, while graciously giving us and those after us a *Saviour* who has *ended war, setting things right in peace*, and since Caesar when revealed surpassed the hopes of all who had anticipated the *good news* [*euangelia*], not only going beyond the benefits of those who had preceded him, but rather leaving no hope of surpassing him for those who will come, because of him *the birthday of God began good news* [*euangelia*] for the world.' (Neil Elliot and Mark Reasoner (eds), *Documents and Images for the Study of Paul* (Minneapolis, MN: Fortress, 2011) p 35, translating lines 32–41; italics added.)